General Editors: Rev. Michael White, Bill Blaul
Editor: Carol N. Abromaitis
Design: Jim Robinson
Photography Coordinator: Mark Swisher
Cover Photograph: Ed Bunyan (*Cardinal greets Pope*)
Frontis Photograph: Mark Swisher (*Crowd gathers*)
Title Page Photograph: Chiaki Kawajiri, The Baltimore Sun (*Pope prays at Basilica*)

Printed and bound in the United States of America, by the John D. Lucas Printing Company.

ISBN-1-885938-01-2 (hc)
ISBN-1-885938-02-0 (pbk)

Library of Congress catalog card number: 95-071402

Cathedral Foundation Press
P.O. Box 777 • Baltimore, Maryland 21203

Publisher: Daniel L. Medinger
Press Director: Gregg A. Wilhelm
Assistant Manager: Patti Medinger

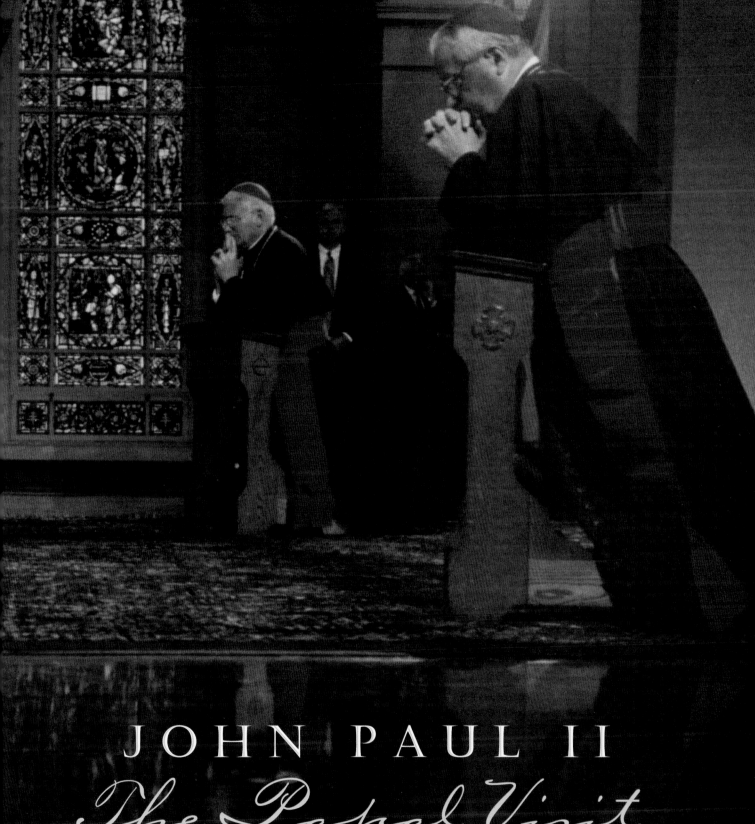

JOHN PAUL II
The Papal Visit
BALTIMORE

*I*n the long and rich history of the Archdiocese of Baltimore, October 8, 1995, takes a place of honor. For a time our city became the world capital of our faith as Pope John Paul II favored us with a most historic visit.

The celebration of the Mass was a high point of a whole array of celebrations reaching up to it and spilling over from it—celebrations at the harbor, in our most venerable churches, museums, and attractions of our city.

Beyond the local attention that the visit captured, the eyes of the world rested on our city and state through vast media coverage. The visit of Pope John Paul II to Baltimore drew the largest public gathering of his U.S. tour, the one in which, as The New York Times reflected, the Pope *"went public"* in a celebration that the Washington Post described as *"part pomp, part pageant, part plain old good fun."* It was *"splendid,"* reflected the Baltimore Sun.

The accompanying volume aims at capturing through the art of photography a variety of perspectives on this great day.

We begin with the preparation, months and months worth by a corps of thousands—volunteers all—captured here in a few visually compelling moments. The energy and excitement of the day's vigil flowed into a unique morning of celebration and song. The day unfolded in scenes of praise and prayer that filled Camden Yards and the streets beyond, Our Daily Bread, the Basilica of the Assumption, the Cathedral of Mary Our

DENISE WALKER

MARK SWISHER

Queen, St. Mary's Seminary and University, and Baltimore/Washington International Airport. For Catholics the day was a defining movement in our history; for all of us it was an unforgettable one, a day of rare autumnal splendor in which our community was charged with a sense of wonder.

William Cardinal Keeler
Archbishop of Baltimore

For the vision
still has its time
and presses on to
fulfillment; it will not
disappoint.

I am weak and I need
Thy strength and power,
To help me over
my weakest hour,

LEGG MASON

P R E P A R A T I O N

DENISE WALKER

It was suggested that someone be assigned to keep count of the hours contributed by volunteer workers.

It was the only position that remained unfilled.

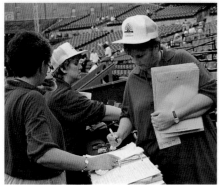
DENISE WALKER

Everything needed for the celebration was provided.

MARK SWISHER

DENISE WALKER

Denise Walker

Denise Walker

Mark Swisher

Denise Walker

Denise Walker

DENISE WALKER

DENISE WALKER

DENISE WALKER

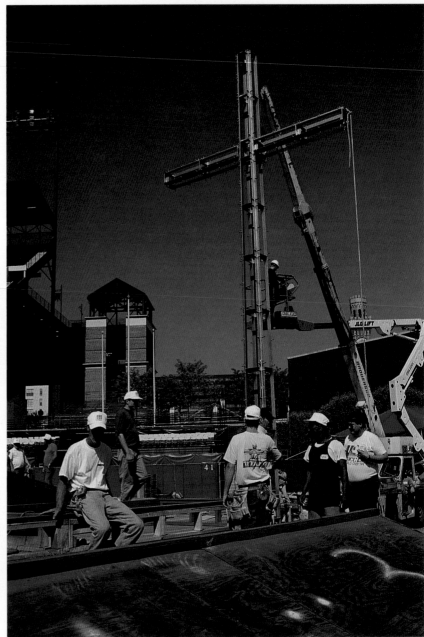

DENISE WALKER

Symbols are the natural speech of a soul, a language older and more universal than words.

C. S. Lewis

MARK SWISHER

Mark Swisher

Mark Swisher

Mark Swisher

Mark Swisher

Mark Swisher

GRANT GURSKY

MARK SWISHER

DENISE WALKER

GRANT GURSKY

The world is charged with
the grandeur of God.
It will flame out like
shining from shook foil.

G. M. Hopkins

EVENING

MARK HEAYN

CELEBRATION

The vigil was kept with a lively program of word and music. The Holy Father's satellite greeting was unexpected as were the brilliant fireworks lifting a celebration of joy and faith to the skies.

John King

All
the stars
were out.

Mark Swisher

Denise Walker

Andrew Campbell

Denise Walker

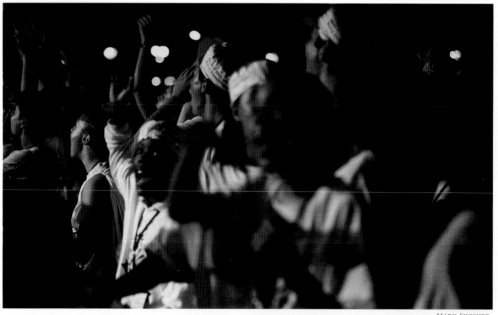

The Young Adult and Youth Corps
worked hard as good will ambassadors
for the weekend events.
They didn't have any trouble relaxing.

MARK SWISHER

MARK SWISHER

GRANT GURSKY

The skies in their
magnificence, the lively,
lovely air...
and all the works of God,
so bright and pure,
so rich and great did seem...

T. Traherne

JOHN KING

MARK HEAYN

*Fill us with
the light of day.*

M O R N I N G

ED BUNYAN

C E L E B R A T I O N

MARK SWISHER

As men and women from across the state gathered at Oriole Park, a celebration of history illustrated by song and dance recalled our diversity, renewed our ties.

MARK LEE

MARK SWISHER

CHUCK SHACOCHIS

CHUCK SHACOCHIS

GRANT GURSKY

GRANT GURSKY

GRANT GURSKY

JEREMY GREEN

CHUCK SHACOCHIS

JOHN KING

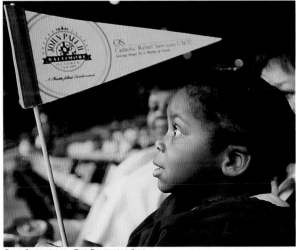

GENE SWEENEY, JR., THE BALTIMORE SUN

MARK SWISHER

Sweet day, so cool, so calm, so bright,

The scoreboard reads "Welcome to Baltimore October 8, 1995"

the bridal of the earth and sky.

G. Herbert

GRANT GURSKY

CHUCK SHACOCHIS

CHUCK SHACOCHIS

AMY DAVIS, THE BALTIMORE SUN

GENE SWEENEY JR., THE BALTIMORE SUN

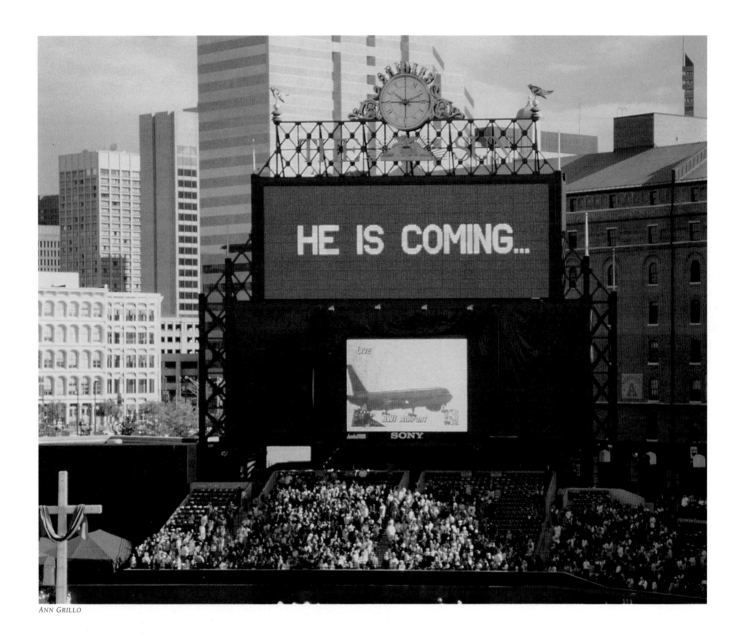

ANN GRILLO

Life will sometimes hand you a magical moment.

Savor it.

*What is
all this juice
and all
this joy?*

G. M. Hopkins

ED BUNYAN

ANN GRILLO

JEREMY GREEN

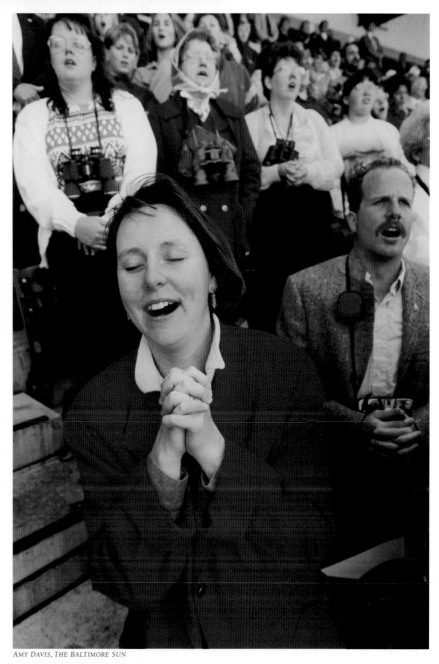

AMY DAVIS, THE BALTIMORE SUN

DENISE WALKER

ED BUNYAN

JEREMY GREEN

DENISE WALKER

DENISE WALKER

DENISE WALKER

GRANT GURSKY

DENISE WALKER

JEREMY GREEN

DENISE WALKER

A pageant full of color recalls the people and events that shaped this first American See.

JEREMY GREEN

MARK LEE

JEREMY GREEN

*The clear vault of the sky
shines forth like heaven itself,
a vision of glory.
The sun resplendent at its rising:
what a wonderful work
of the Lord it is.*

The Morning Celebration was

GRANT GURSKY

MATT SPANGLER

DENISE WALKER

a joint effort — eventually.

GRANT GURSKY

MARK LEE

MARK SWISHER

DAVE TILLMAN

AP/ WIDE WORLD PHOTOS

DAVE TILLMAN

Thousands cheer as the Holy Father in his unique car moves around Camden Yards.

AP/ WIDE WORLD PHOTOS

DENISE WALKER

DENISE WALKER

JOHN HOUSER

GRANT GURSKY

KARL MERTON FERRON, THE BALTIMORE SUN

The heavens proclaim
the glory of God,
and all creation
is shouting for joy.

ED BUNYAN

M   A   S   S

LARRY GALLOWAY

ED BUNYAN

The Mass was the center and the high point of a day in which inherent holiness was manifest in simplicity and splendor.

CHUCK SHACOCHIS

GRANT GURSKY

ED BUNYAN

Ed Bunyan

Larry Galloway

Ed Bunyan

Denise Walker

Mark Swisher

Mark Lee

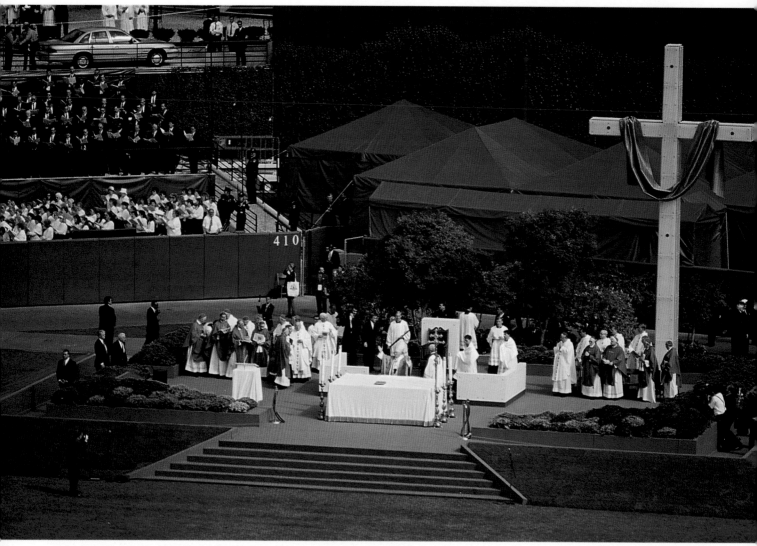

MARK SWISHER

Nature is never spent.
There lives the dearest freshness
deep down things.

G. M. Hopkins

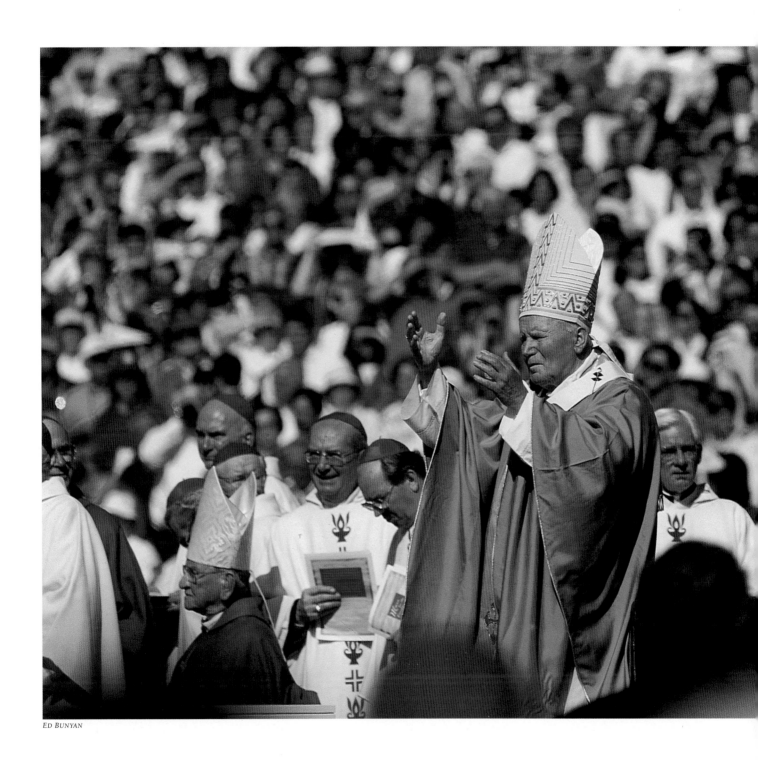

ED BUNYAN

Behold the glory of
the Lord filled the house.

ED BUNYAN

The thought of God... is the happiness of man.

Cardinal Newman

MARK LEE

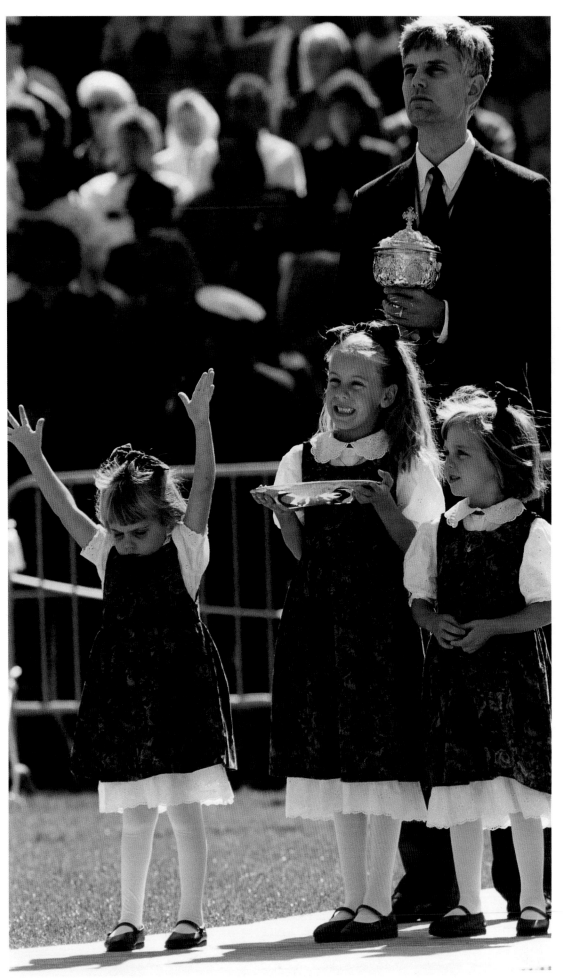

JED KIRSCHBAUM, THE BALTIMORE SUN

ED BUNYAN

ED BUNYAN

ED BUNYAN

The Lord is good
to those who hope in Him,

to those who are searching

for His love.

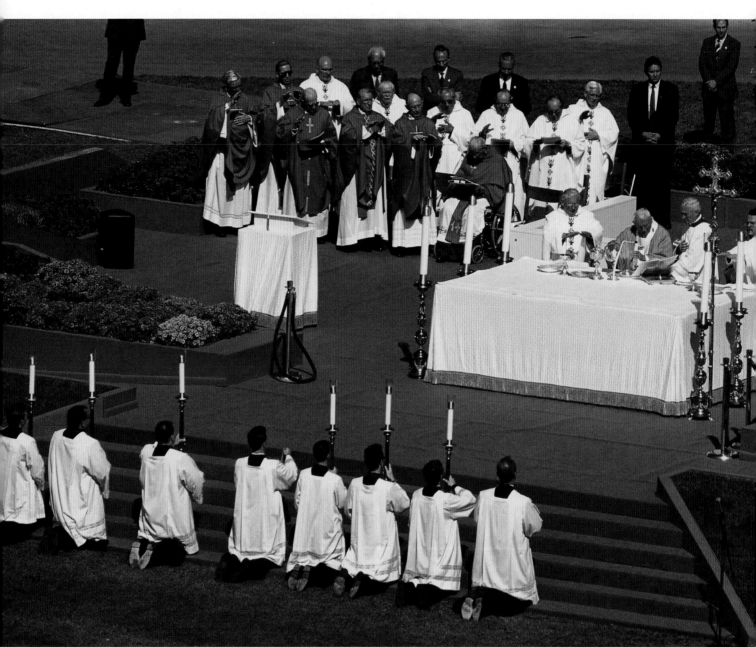

GRANT GURSKY

FACING PHOTO: JEREMY GREEN

Next to the Blessed Sacrament itself,

*your neighbor is the holiest object
presented to your sense.*

C. S. Lewis

MARK LEE

MARK LEE

MARK LEE

MARK LEE

MARK LEE

AMY DAVIS, THE BALTIMORE SUN

Let your light shine before men,
that they may see
your good works and give glory
to your Father in Heaven.

THE PARADE

MARK HEAYN

ANDREA CIPRIANI

AP/ WIDE WORLD PHOTOS

ANDREA CIPRIANI

JOHN KING

KENNETH K. LAM, THE BALTIMORE SUN

ANDREA CIPRIANI

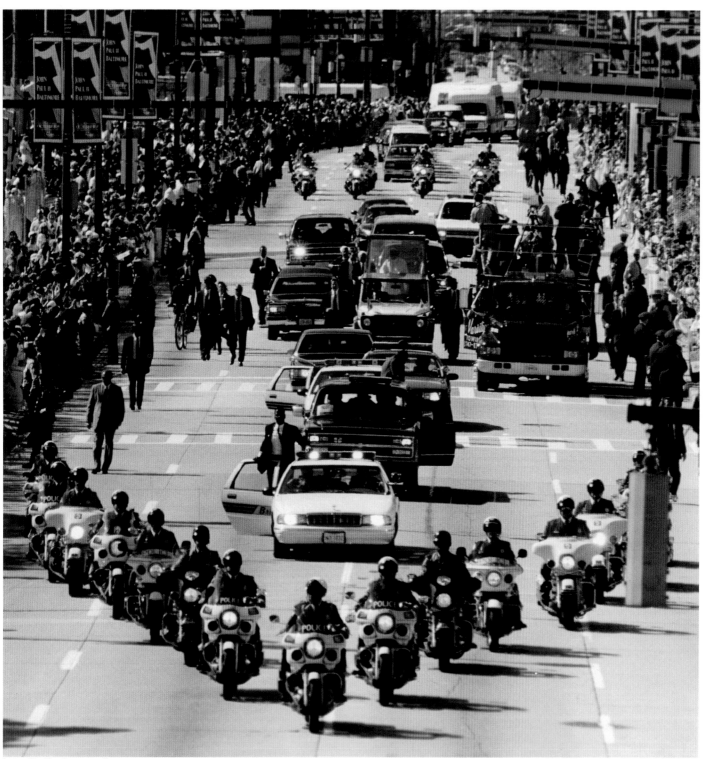

LLOYD FOX, THE BALTIMORE SUN

Chuck Shacochis

Chuck Shacochis

Chuck Shacochis

Chuck Shacochis

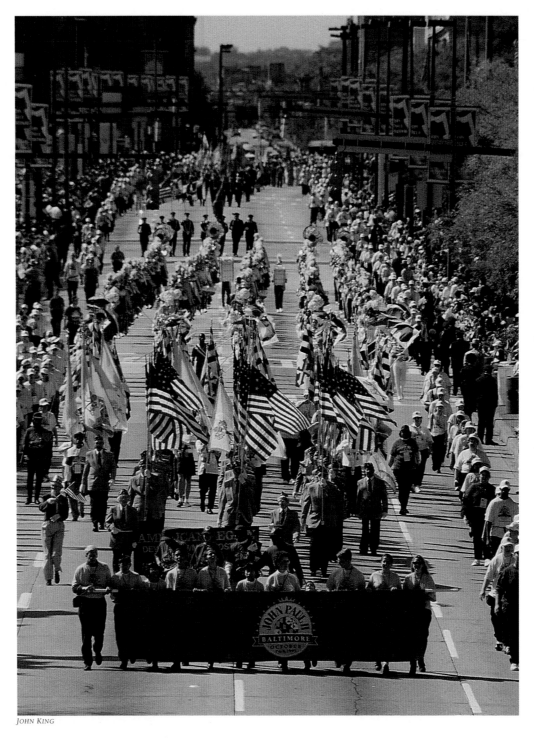

JOHN KING

To carry the massive parade banner,
the Daly family was asked to
lend a hand — 22 actually.

MARSHALL CLARKE

CHUCK SHACOCHIS

JOHN KING

MARSHALL CLARKE

JOHN KING

MARSHALL CLARKE

*Of the thousands
who marched
in the parade,
many had
a good time.*

ANDREA CIPRIANI

JEREMY GREEN

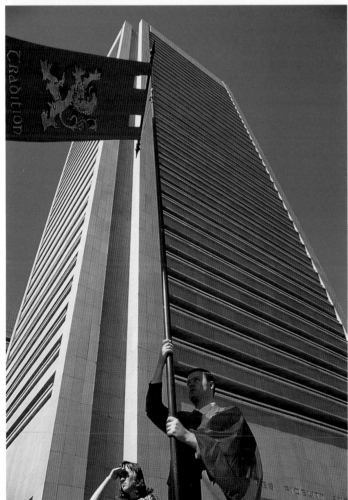

ANDREA CIPRIANI

ANDREA CIPRIANI

*Most had
a great time.*

...The streets I trod,
the lit straight
streets shot out and
met the
starry streets that
point to God.

G.K. Chesterton

JOHN KING

ANDREA CIPRIANI

JOHN KING

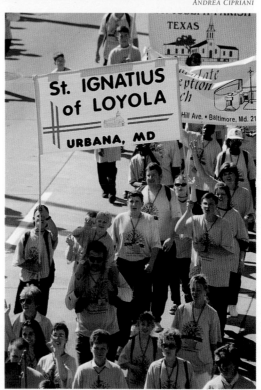

JOHN KING

FACING PHOTO: MARSHALL CLARKE

Thou art Peter,
and upon this rock
I will build my Church.

Chiaki Kawajiri, The Baltimore Sun

WITH HIS PEOPLE

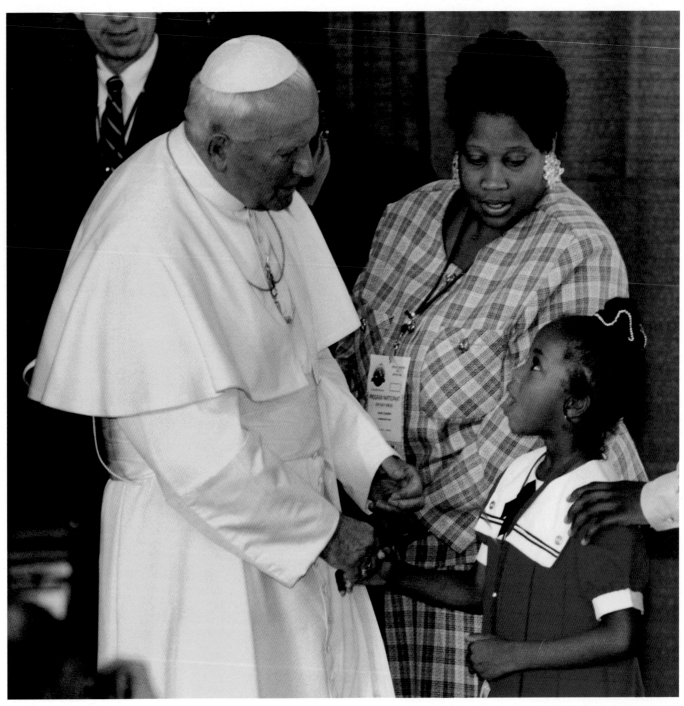

GEORGE W. HOLSEY, THE BALTIMORE SUN

Brittany Campbell, age 6, affectionately greets the successor of Saint Peter as "Uncle Pope."

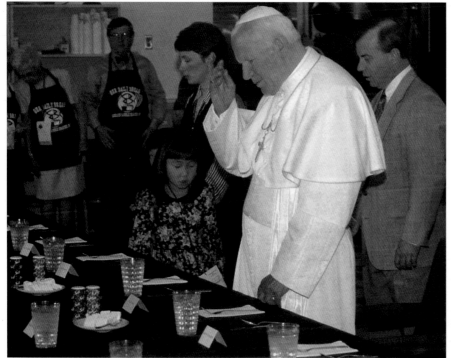

AP/ Wide World Photos

Our Daily Bread

Mark Swisher

Mark Swisher

Mark Swisher

The Basilica

OUR DAILY BREAD

Prayer does not
change God,
but it changes
him who prays.
S. Kierkegaard

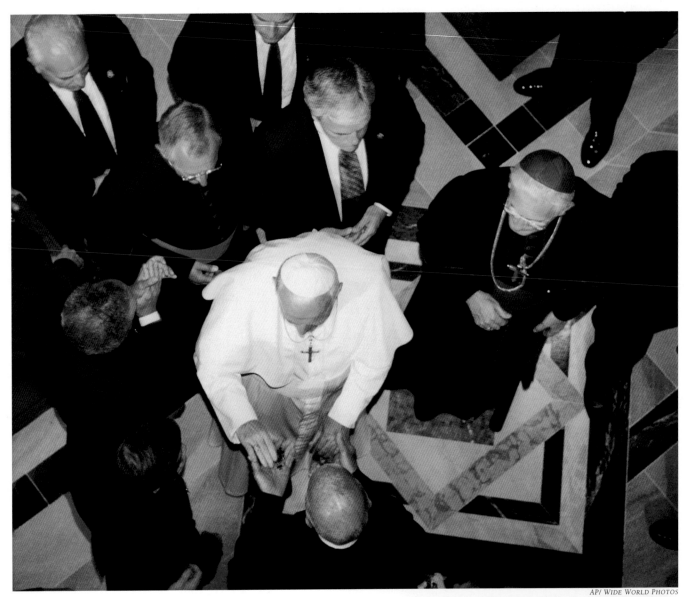

Cathedral of Mary Our Queen

CHIEN-CHI CHANG, THE BALTIMORE SUN

DEAN ALEXANDER

DENISE WALKER

SAL DI MARCO, JR.

He has made everything beautiful in its time; also he has put eternity into man's mind.

SAL DI MARCO, JR.

SAL DI MARCO, JR.

MARK HEAYN

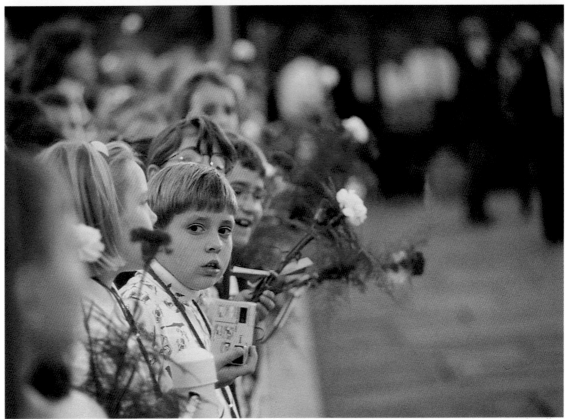

JOHN KING

Harmony,
heavenly harmony

J. Dryden

MARK HEAYN

MARK HEAYN

MARK HEAYN

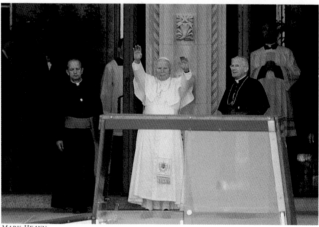

MARK HEAYN

St. Mary's Seminary

St. Mary's Seminary was established in 1791.

JEREMY GREEN

*The first visit by a Pope to the
nation's first seminary didn't
come a moment too soon.*

Grant Gursky

Grant Gursky

So call the
field to rest and
let's away,

To part the
glories of this
happy day.

W. Shakespeare

The Archdiocese of Baltimore,
Catholic Charities,
the Basilica National Shrine,
the Cathedral of Mary Our
Queen, St. Mary's Seminary
and University, and the
many hundreds who planned
for Pope John Paul II's visit,
wish to thank
a few of our friends.

The City of Baltimore,
Kurt L. Schmoke, Mayor
The State of Maryland,
Parris Glendening, Governor
Baltimore City Department of Public Works
Baltimore City Department of Recreation
and Parks
Baltimore City Fire Department
Baltimore City Life Museum
Baltimore City Police Department
Baltimore Museum of Art
Baltimore Office of Promotion
Baltimore Orioles Baseball Club
Baltimore Symphony Orchestra
Baltimore/Washington
International Airport
Columbus Center
Enoch Pratt Free Library
Evergreen House Foundation
Great Blacks in Wax Museum
Harborplace and The Gallery
Homewood House Museum
Maryland Department of Transportation
Maryland Emergency Management Agency
Maryland Historical Society
Maryland Stadium Authority
Maryland State Police
Mass Transit Administration
National Aquarium at Baltimore
United States Department of Defense
United States Postal Service
United States Secret Service
The Walters Art Gallery
World Trade Center: Top of the World
Observation Museum

SPECIAL BENEFACTORS

Mr. and Mrs. James C. Alban III
Mr. and Mrs. Michael J. Batza
Mr. and Mrs. Richard O. Berndt
Mr. and Mrs. J. P. Blase Cooke

Mr. C. Edward Jones
Mr. and Mrs. Earl L. Linehan
Mr. and Mrs. Louis V. Manzo

MAJOR CORPORATE SPONSORS

ARA-Mark
Baltimore Gas and Electric Company
BMW North America
Bon Secours Health System, Inc.
Bon Secours Hospital
Cardinal Shehan Center
Catholic Relief Services
Cellular One
Coca-Cola Company
Cochran, Stephenson & Donkervoet
Incorporated
Franciscan Health System
Good Samaritan Hospital
Peggy and Yale Gordon Trust
Harkins Builders, Inc.
Jewish Chautauqua Society
Kodak
Land Rover North America
Loyola College in Maryland
Nick and Mary Mangione of Turf Valley
Resort and Conference Center
Mercy Medical Center
Morgan Creek Productions
Mount St. Mary's College and Seminary
Raskob Foundation for
Catholic Activities, Inc.
St. Agnes Health Care
St. Joseph Medical Center
San Pellegrino
Sheraton Inner Harbor Hotel
TWA
Zambelli Internationale Fireworks

SPECIAL SPONSORS

American Stone Mix
Bell Atlantic
Benziger Publishing Company
Bethesda Engravers
The T. Talbott Bond Company
Brass Elephant Restaurant
Black & Decker
Central Parking
College of Notre Dame of Maryland
Crown Central Petroleum Corp.
Federal Armored Express
First Fidelity, N.A.
First National Bank of Maryland
Graham Landscape Architects

Hecht's
Holy Name Union
The Inn at Pier V
Jade Farm Sod House
Knights of Columbus, Maryland State
Council
Legg Mason, Inc.
Maestro Gilbert Levine
Loane Brothers, Inc.
Luskin's
Macy's
Mark Downs Office Furniture
Marriott Corp.
Marriott Hotel BWI
Martin's Eastpoint
Martin's Northpoint
Martin's West
Maryland Office Relocators, Inc.
Mid-Atlantic Coca-Cola Bottling Co.
NationsBank
PageNet
R. A. Daffer & Sons
Restaurant Assn. of Maryland
RJ Sunday Landscaping, Inc.
Rodgers Instrument Corporation
Ruck Funeral Homes
The House of Seagram
Smith Marine Towing
Southpaw Entertainment
Harry M. Stevens, Inc.
Stouffer Harborplace Hotel
Sun Micro Systems, Inc.
Swann/Hall Associates Ltd.
Synergetic Concepts
Whitaker Bros. Business Group
Whiting-Turner Contracting Company

SPONSORS

American Cafe
American Red Cross
Apex
Arby's Roast Beef Restaurants
Archbishop Curley High School
Archbishop Spalding High School
Babe Ruth Museum
Balloons Over America
Baltimore Office Relocators
Baltimore Trolley Tours
Baltimore Zoo
Barbera Business Systems
William Beck & Son
Beer Institute
Bello-Vitto's Pizza
Ben & Jerry's Homemade Ice Cream

Benfield Florists
Biddle Street Caterers
Blockbusters
A Blooming Basket
Bode Floors & Carpets
Brick Oven Pizza
BWI Florist
BWI Operations
Calvert Associates, Inc.
Calvert Hall College
Cameo Caterers
Captain James Landing
Cardinal Gibbons School
Carpentry & Hardware Services, Inc.
Casa di Pasta
Chart House
Chef's Expressions
Chesapeake Wholesale Florist, Inc.
Chopticon High School Band
City College High School Band
Classic Catering People
Coach House Restaurant
Comcast Cablevision
Communications
Equipment, Inc., of Timonium
Continental Baking Company
Convention Store
Country Club of Maryland
Crumbs Galore
Dale's Flowers
Day's Inn Inner Harbor
Desserts by Design
DiTech Group
Domino Sugar
Domino's Pizza
Double T Diner
Dunkin' Donuts
Emery Worldwide
Entenmann's
Eyre Bus Service
Farm Fresh
Fenwick Bakery
Filippo's Pizzeria
Freestate, Inc.
Fuddruckers
Garland's Garden Center
Germano's
Giant Foods
Gibbons of Baltimore
Giovanni's
Grandma Utz
Louis J. Grasmick Lumber Co., Inc.
J. F. Grottendick and Sons
H&S Bakery

H&S Lumber
Harbor Court Hotel
Harborside
Hawai'i Aloha Lu'au Dancers & Catering
Holiday Inn Inner Harbor
Holy Cross Parish, Baltimore
Horn & Horn Smorgasbord
Hostess Cakes
Jefferson and Jones
Jefferson Smurfit Corporation
John Carroll School
Journey's Rest Farm
KMart Stores
Lauman's Fine Furniture
Luigi Petti
Maryland Bible Society
Maryland Fence
Manufacturing Company, Inc.
Maryland Science Center
Donald McKinney and
Carole Deegan-McKinney
Metro
Metro Food Market/Basics
Metro Traffic Control
Miller and Long
Morganza High School Band
Mother Hubbard's Cupboard
Mount deSales Academy
Mount St. Joseph High School
Na Fianna Irish Pipe Band
Office Depot
Victor Ostrowski & Son, Inc.
Otterbein's Bakery
Our Lady of Perpetual Help Parish,
Ilchester
Our Lady of the Chesapeake Parish,
Pasadena
The Palm Restaurant
Paoli's Restaurant
Papa John's Pizza International, Inc.
Papa Leone's Spaghetti House
Paramount Limousine Service
Paramount Restaurant
Penske Truck Rental & Leasing
Perzynski & Filar Florist
Pete's Pizza
Phillips Restaurant
Pizza Hut
Power Bar
Price Club White Marsh
Price-Modern, Inc.
Geo. W. Radebaugh & Sons, Inc.
Radisson Plaza Lord Baltimore Hotel
Edward G. Rahll & Sons
Red Lobster Restaurants

Results, Inc.
Roy Rogers Family Restaurants
Sabatino's Italian Restaurant
Safeway
St. Jerome Parish
St. Jude Shrine
St. Michael the Archangel Parish, Overlea
Santoni's Markets
Scoops and Slices
Seton Keough High School
Shamrock Engraving of Glen Burnie
Silver Burdett
Sir Speedy Printing Center of Columbia
Sisters of the Visitation, Frederick
Sizzler Restaurants
Southern Maryland Trailer
Squire's Restaurant & Catering
Stonyfield Yogurt
Strapazza Restaurant
Summitville Baltimore, Inc.
Taco Bell
Tamburo, Inc.
That's Amore
Thrifty Car Rental
Tiralla's, Inc.
Total Audio Visual Systems, Inc.
Totes, Incorporated
Turf Valley Country Club
United Parcel Service
United States Fidelity & Guaranty
University of Maryland Marching Band
Valley Florals & Treats
Valu Food Supermarkets
Tony Vitrano Co.
Von Paris Moving & Storage Co.
WalMart Stores
Wendy's
Williams Crane Service, Inc.
Roger Wittenbach, Inc.
Wolfe's Restaurant
Woodward & Lothrop Department Store,
White Marsh Mall
Yellow Cab

Quotations from *Lectionary for Mass.* Copyright ©1970
by the Confraternity of Christian Doctrine.
Washington, D.C. Reprinted with permission.

Quotations from C.S. Lewis, *Studies in Medieval and
Renaissance Literature.* Copyright ©1966 by the
Cambridge University Press. New York.
Reprinted with permission.

The poems of Gerard Manly Hopkins are copyrighted
by the English Province of the Society of Jesus.

Quotations from the *Douay-Rheims Bible.* Copyright
©1940 by the Confraternity of Christian Doctrine.
Washington, D.C. Reprinted with permission.

PHOTO BY SAL DI MARCO, JR.

AP/ WIDE WORLD PHOTOS

*We thank you God
for this most amazing day.*